A marvelous sunset over **St. Peter's Square**. Very few states in the world can boast a vestibule like that created by St. Peter's Square.

THE COLOURS OF
ROME

IMAGES OF THE SITES,
AROMAS AND MEMORIES
OF THE ETERNAL CITY

ROME THROUGH THE CENTURIES

ANCIENT ROME

Tradition has it that Rome was founded by Romulus, the first king, in 753 BC. More than a millennium passed from its birth to its decline, which followed the first waves of barbarian invasion. What can still be admired today in almost every corner of the city center are mainly ruins dating from the Republican age, which began with the expulsion of the last King, Tarquin the Proud (509 BC) and especially the remains of the subsequent Imperial age, which lasted from the rule of Augustus (27 AD) to that of Romulus Augustulus (476). The changes Rome has undergone through its history of over 2750 years have not effaced the traces left by time. While temples of the Republican period may be seen in the sacred area of Largo di Torre Argentina or near the Foro Boario, Imperial Rome reveals itself in its full splendor in the area of the Roman Forum, the Palatine and the imperial Forums, with the incomparable outline of the Coliseum in the background.

CHRISTIAN ROME

It was a Roman emperor, Constantine (fourth century) who initiated the building of the first great Christian basilicas such as St John the Lateran, St Lawrence outside the Walls and above all St Peter s in the Vatican. In the following century, the Church began to gain enough strength and autonomy to begin the construction of basilicas which are now well-known places of worship. The basilicas of St Mary Major and St. Paul date from this period. The Rome of the popes also grew by adapting and transforming the pre-existing buildings to the needs of worship, using the enormous quantity of marble, metal and other materials these monuments provided. The celebration of the Church s spiritual and temporal primacy paved the way to the urban rebirth of Rome which began in the Middle Ages and was fully established by the beginning of the 15th century.

From that time, all the pontiffs, such as Nicholas V, who planned the demolition of the Constantinian Basilica of St Peter in order to build the new one, or Julius II, who commissioned works by Michelangelo and Rafael, strove to increase the magnificence of their pontificates.

From Renaissance Rome to the 19th century

The continuation of the Church's great influence in the European courts gave rise to a flourishing urban rebirth from the second half of the 15th century. In this time important construction projects were accomplished for the nobility, such as the building of a palace for Cardinal Farnese in 1516, the reorganization of the Capitol, entrusted to Michelangelo by Paul III in 1536, the construction of villas with gardens, squares, such as Campo de' Fiori and Piazza Farnese, streets such as Via Giulia and a new network of roads conceived by Pope Sixtus V. Renaissance architectural plans were modeled on examples of classical art, based on strict geometrical proportions. Bernini and Borromini, both Baroque architects, gave new shapes to fountains, façades, churches and squares, as can be seen in the spectacular Piazza Navona. The 18th century, on the other hand, was marked by the building of works with a great urban impact, of which the Trevi Fountain (1732) and the Spanish Steps (1735) are outstanding examples. From the Baroque, the fashion in the early 19th century reverted to the more simple Neoclassical structures, in the wake of the rediscovery of classical antiquity in all its forms.

Modern Rome

The proclamation, in 1870, of Rome as the capital of the Kingdom of Italy led to radical changes. The transfer to the city of the royal court, the parliament and the ministries, gave rise to an immediate increase in the population and upset the tranquil atmosphere of papal Rome. Between the end of the 19th century and the first decades of the 20th, works such as the Victor Emanuel II monument were inaugurated, to whose grandiose proportions irreplaceable historical and artistic monuments were sacrificed. The prevalent style in this period was Neo-Renaissance, flanked by Art Nouveau and perennial Neoclassicism. Whole neighborhoods were built, such as the Ludovisi district, with the famous Via Veneto, on the site of the splendid villa which bore that name. Later the imperial aspirations of the Fascist regime (1922/43) produced architectural works inspired by ancient Rome. In this period, further demolition of old mediaeval and Renaissance neighborhoods was carried out to make room for roads such as the Via dei Fori Imperiali, and the Via della Conciliazione. At the same time, plans for the expansion of the urban fabric toward the sea were established; in this context the EUR quarter was built.

The **Via Sacra**. Shining columns reach upwards near the Arch of Titus, and old stones worn smooth by time.

Right, the **Roman Forum**. The center of civic and economic life in Republican times, the Forum maintained an important role also in the Imperial period.

The **Arch of Constantine** was built by the Senate at the edge of the Forum, in memory of the victory over Maxentius at Ponte Milvio (312 AD).

Left, the **Roman Forum**. The **Temple of Saturn** (498 BC). It was always used as the public treasury. On the right three columns remain of the **Temple of Vespasian** (94 AD).

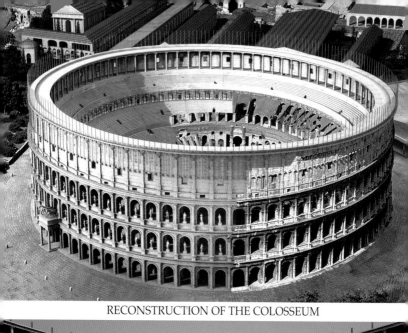

RECONSTRUCTION OF THE COLOSSEUM

The **Colosseum**. This immense amphitheater was begun by Vespasian in 72 AD and completed by his son Titus in 80 AD. Its true name is the "Flavian Amphitheater".

It was commonly called the *Colosseum*, both for its proportions and its vicinity to the Colossus of Nero.

The *Colosseum* had the same function as a modern giant stadium, but the favorite spectacles in Roman times were the games of the Circus (*ludi circenses*). This was the origin of the professional gladiators, who were trained to fight to the death, while wild beasts of every sort increased the horror of the show. The Colosseum is elliptical in shape, 187 meters at its longest end and 155 meters at its shortest. The height of the external ring reaches 50 meters from ground level. It was designed to accommodate an estimated 60,000 spectators. Around the exterior run three orders of arches, respectively adorned with Doric, Ionian and Corinthian columns.

Trajan's Markets located between Trajan's Forum and the lower slopes of the Quirinal, are magnificently preserved.

Right, the beautiful **Egyptian obelisk** erected on Quirinale Hill between two colossal Roman-era groups of **horse breakers**.

The **Pantheon** is the city's only architecturally intact monument from classical times. It was destroyed by a fire in 80 AD, and completely redesigned by Hadrian.

On March 16, 609 AD, Pope Boniface IV changed the *Pantheon* into a Christian church, bringing the bones of many Christians from the catacombs.

Castel Sant'Angelo. What looks like an impregnable fortress was created by the Emperor Hadrian as his tomb.

The Mole of Hadrian, now *Castel Sant'Angelo*, was begun in 123 AD and held the remains of the Imperial family until Caracalla (217 AD).

The **Appian Way** is the Roman road which has the greatest number of interesting archaeological, artistic and natural features. It was begun by Claudius in 312 BC.

Right, aerial view of the **Isola Tiberina**, where the church of St. Bartholomew stands on the ruins of the celebrated Temple of Aesculapius, the Greek God of medicine.

The **Basilica di San Clemente** is among the most interesting churches in Rome from both an artistic and historical point of view.

Right, **Santa Maria in Cosmedin** stands on the ruins of a Temple to Hercules. On the left side of the portico is a marble mask called the Bocca della Verità.

St. Peter's Basilica. Michelangelo's mighty silver-blue dome dominates the scene, blending into the sky above. The colonnade is Bernini's most beautiful work.

The dome of St. Peter's cupola towers powerfully against the backdrop of the sky and its grey-blue colour blends into the very same hue of the sky.

Above the altar rises Bernini's fantastic *baldacchino* (1633), supported by four spiral columns, made from bronze taken from the Pantheon.

But the glorification of the tomb of the humble fisherman from Galilee is the majestic *dome* that soars toward the heavens.

Left, the *high altar*, under the cupola, rises above the *Tomb* of St. Peter, which was definitively identified after excavations in the 1950's.

The Borghese Pope Paul V commissioned Maderno (1607-1614) to construct the broad *façade* of the church. The two fountains, the one on the right designed by Maderno (1613) and the one on the left by Carlo Fontana (1675), harmonize beautifully with the vast square.

Michelangelo was already quite old (1546) when he began the project of the dome and when he died (1564) only the drum had been completed.

Right, in the first chapel of the right nave is Michelangelo's **Pietà**, sculpted between 1498 and 1499..

San Giovanni in Laterano, the Cathedral of Rome, was founded by Constantine, during the papacy of St. Sylvester (314-335).

Right, the vastness of the central nave has as a background an imposing tabernacle (late 14th century).

The *Basilica di San Paolo* with its Vassalletto's **Cosmatesque Cloister** (restored in 1907), is among the most significant examples of Roman marble work.

Left, the *inside* of the Basilica di San Paolo is opulent and impressive. The Gothic Style *canopy* is a 13th century masterpiece by Arnolfo di Cambio.

The *Basilica di San Pietro in Vincoli*. In the basilica is the tomb of Pope Julius II by Michelangelo. At the center is the statue of **Moses**.

Left, the **Basilica of Santa Maria Maggiore**, the fourth largest church in Rome, is the only basilica which still retains its original shape and character.

Piazza del Campidoglio was designed by Michelangelo. The old artist placed on a new pedestal the equestrian statue of the Emperor Marcus Aurelius (161-180).

Right, an aerial view of the **Capitol**. The square was designed by Michelangelo for the magnificent Pope Paul III (1534-1549) and it was conceived as a vast terrace opening on the city.

Piazza Navona, or Circus Agonale, traces the shape of the Stadium of Domitian, which once occupied this site and held 30,000 spectators.

Piazza Naavona. In the center is the Fountain of the Four Rivers, at the south end is the **Fountain of the Moor** and on the north side is the Fountain of the Neptune.

Campo de' Fiori, with its lively daily market is still a typical corner of old Rome today.

Left, a charming photo of Piazza Navona at dawn. A close-up of one of the three fountains in the square: the **Fountain of Neptune**.

Fontana di Trevi. Set against a large building, the fountain is decorated with bas-reliefs and statues that stand upon mighty rocks from which the water gushes. In the center of the *Fontana di Trevi*, the Statue of Oceanus standing on a shell drawn by sea horses.
The *Fontana di Trevi* was built by Nicola Salvi (1735) under Pope Clement XII, and was decorated by several followers of Bernini.

Piazza di Spagna. At the top of the steps is the **church of the Trinità dei Monti**, with its two cupolas (1495), and an Egyptian obelisk in front, brought here from the Sallustian Gardens in 1789.

The staircase built by Francesco de Santis, starting in 1723, is made up of 138 steps. At the foot of the staircase of Trinità dei Monti, the **"Spanish Steps"**, we find the **Fontana della Barcaccia** (1629) by Pietro Bernini, father of Gian Lorenzo.

Via Giulia. A long street built by Pope Julius II in the 16th century to replace the winding narrow streets that previously linked the Vatican to the Capitol.

The **Gianicolo** which offers some of the finest views of the city. On the great panoramic piazza is a monument to Giuseppe Garibaldi by Gallori (1895).

The Casino Borghese is the site of the **Borghese Museum** and **Gallery**. It was built by the Dutch architect Van Santen (Vasanzio) in 1613, and restored in 1782 by M. Borghese.

Right, **Villa Borghese.** Shaded by the lofty trees in the most secret recess of the *Giardino del Lago*, a little classic-style temple is reflected in the green waters of an artificial lake.

Via Veneto is known for its elegance. Via Veneto, the road in front of Villa Borghese park, is a symbol of the "dolce vita" that characterized life in the capital during the 60s.

Right, **Piazza della Repubblica.** Initially called Piazza Esedra because of its shape which follows the curve of the exedra of the ancient Baths of Diocletian.

The **Palazzo della Civiltà e del Lavoro** in the EUR district, built between 1938 and 1943, is commonly called the "square Colosseum" for the 216 arches that characterize its four broad façades.

Left, the **Vittorio Emanuele II Monument**, was designed by Sacconi (1885-1911). In the center is the *Altar of the Fatherland*, crowned by the *statue of Rome*, at whose feet since 1921 lies the Tomb of the Unknown Soldier.

© LOZZI ROMA S.A.S.
THE COLOURS OF ROME

ISBN: 978-88-89896-39-6

Editor:
LOZZI ROMA s.a.s.
Via Filippo Nicolai, 91
00136 Roma (Italy)
Tel. (+39) 06 35497051
06 97841668
Fax (+39) 06 35497074 ·
E-mail: info@lozziroma.com
Web: www.gruppolozzi.it

Printed by:
CSC Grafica s.r.l. - Guidonia (Roma)
E-mail: info@cscgrafica.it
Web: www.cscgrafica.it

Photographs:
Lozzi Roma s.a.s.
Millenium s.r.l.

Archivio Fotografico della
Fabbrica di San Pietro
Scala Archives - Firenze

MADE IN ITALY